10 Minute University

10 MINUTE UNIVERSITY

The World's Fastest-Talking Man Teaches the World's Greatest Lessons

Jim Becker, Andy Mayer, Bob Tzudiker and Noni White

Performed by John "Mighty Mouth" Moschitta

Illustrations by Mark Brewer

BARNES
& NOBLE
BOOKS
NEW YORK

This edition published by Barnes & Noble, Inc., by arrangement with becker&mayer!
2004 Barnes & Noble Books
M 10 9 8 7 6 5 4 3 2 1

Editorial: Conor Risch
Design: Todd Bates
Production coordination: Leah Finger
Project management: Sheila Kamuda

ISBN 0-7607-5555-8

Library of Congress Cataloging-in-Publication data is available.

Printed in Malaysia

CONTENTS

ORiENTATiON

Welcome students. As you embark on your COLLEGE EDUCATiON at 10 Minute University, you will be receiving an education unavailable at even the finest of institutions. At TMU you will learn more in ten minutes than you would in four years of traditional college. For the Bachelor of Arts degree, it is required that you study BiOLOGY, PSYCHOLOGY, PHiLOSOPHY, FiLM APPRECiATiON, CONVERSATiONAL LATiN, PHYSiCS, COMPARATiVE LiTERATURE, ECONOMiCS, AND FOOTBALL. Welcome to college—THE TEN BEST MiNUTES OF YOUR LiFE.

BiOLOGy 103:

THE THEORY OF EVOLUTiON

I'm a mutant. You're a mutant. WE'RE ALL MUTANTS. And in Biology 103: The Theory of Evolution, we investigate the evolutionary process over the last 3.5 billion years. It will take just a minute to explain.

E verywhere you look these days there are birds, bees, bacteria, beagles. It wasn't always that way. ONCE THERE WAS ONLY SLOP. Primordial slop. Some self-replicating molecules started replicating and that's life. From a bunch of DNA in the goo, you get brain surgeons and BMWs in just a few billions years. How? NATURAL SELECTION. Survival of the fittest. Who are the fittest? The ones who survive. Inter-specific competition determines success within the species. Take puffballs. Say puffier puffballs mean tougher puffballs. The puffballs with the right stuff pass their tough stuff on through their offspring

because PUFFINESS IS A HERITABLE TRAIT. The fecund fungus' offspring get puffier and puffier while its scrawny fellow fungus bites the dust. But that's life. Heritable traits that work, work. The ones that don't, don't. That's why fish have flippers not feet. FISH WITH FEET DIED. So how does one species become another? They mutate. Take primates. Natural selection selected some simians who stood up straighter—that's us. Better posture meant more dates, more sex, more reproduction, and soon we had a gene pool of our own. Very exclusive. NO MORE FRATERNIZING WITH UNCLE MONKEY. But that's life. Once you've got your own species, sexual selection takes over. Some traits are sexier to the opposite sex. Take fruit flies: Some have red eyes, some have white eyes. Girl fruit flies flip for guys with red eyes, furthering the demise of the guys with white eyes. NATURAL SELECTION SURE IS FUN WHEN YOU'RE THE SURVIVOR. One day everything's great. You're surviving and sexually selective. The next thing you know a million years have gone by and you're dead. But hey, that's life.

PSYCHOLOGY 1:

● ● ● ● ● ● ● ● ● ● ● ●

INTRODUCTION TO PSYCHOLOGY

Psychology is the systematic study of behavior and the factors that influence it. In Psychology 1, we will learn how to identify and correctly label other people's SICK, NEUROTIC, PATHETIC BEHAVIOR.

et's take a look at BETTY: a caring mother and devoted wife who believes that the family dog was sent from outer space to conduct sadistic mind control experiments on her children. Betty's not playing with a FULL DECK. That's because Betty is a paranoid personality. Why? Betty is insane.

14

And then there's Bob. Happy-go-lucky one day, kills his mother the next. Bob is a psychotic manic depressive. Why did he do that? BECAUSE HE'S INSANE. And how about all those people who are addicted to WHEEL OF FORTUNE? Obsessive-compulsive behavior or just insane? Freud would say it's the work of the UNCONSCIOUS MIND comprised of the sex-starved warmonger id, and the goody goody superego. But does that really explain these behaviors? Who knows? Or maybe it's because the brain is made up of 10 billion itty-bitty, teeny-weeny nerve cells. And what happens when just one of those little cells steps out of line? You guessed it. MALFUNCTION IN THE CEREBRAL CORTEX. We're talking hallucinations, schizophrenia, and before you know it, it's frontal lobotomy time. Let's look at the research. Take white rats, two groups. The experimental group is given a hundred milligrams pure LSD and receives 50-volt intermittent ELECTRICAL SHOCKS, via electrodes implanted in the brain, for ten weeks as they negotiate a complex maze while deprived of water, food, and sex. The control group is given a PLACEBO much as Ozzy and Harriet reruns on TV. When we look at the mean or the median or the mode we see that our experimental subjects have developed stomach ulcers, hypersensitivity to all stimuli, and are suicidal schizophrenic. What does this prove? THE RATS ARE TOTALLY INSANE.

Mr. Socrates

PHILOSOPHY 201:

● ● ● ● ● ● ● ● ● ● ●

THE STUDY OF EPISTEMOLOGY

This is Philosophy 201: The Study of Epistemology, in which we ask: How do we know what we know when we know that we know it even if we don't know if we really know it? THIS IS NOT AN EASY COURSE.

How about the tree in the quad? Does that tree really exist? Am I here? How do I know? ARE YOU THERE? If so, are you awake? And what if I don't see the tree? Is it still there? In other words, is the universe really the SOLIPSISTIC EXTENSION OF SELFHOOD OVER THE APPARENT PHENOMENA? If phenomena come from you and numina come from me, what does that do to the unseen tree in the quad? GOT IT? Good. So what is knowing? Do I know? What if hypothesize I don't know? A-ha! Then I do know something! Or do I? Stay with me here. I know that I do not know so it is possible to know—in the Socratic sense of knowing—the lack of knowledge. But IS THERE AN I INVOLVED WHEN I SAY I? Is Descartes right when he says "COGNITO ERGO SUM"—I think, therefore I am? Couldn't I just be a bunch of sensations with an illusion of I? Is it possible I don't exist at all or you don't exist? Is thinking dreaming and dreaming nightmarish and NOTHING EXISTS? Wait a second. Do you need a priori knowledge to know that that tree exists? What if I try walking through it on my way to lunch? Wouldn't a simple appeal to cause and effect free us from the conundrum of subjective idealism? Can I CREAM MY HEAD on a nonexistent tree when I don't even know that my head is in your head dreaming that it's my head saying "COGNITO ERGO SUM," as opposed to a real tree raising a real welt on my, and I mean *my* head, thus NEGATING A NEED FOR NUMINA in a nightmarish world not in my own making? GOT IT?

ROMAN STUDIES 25:

● ● ● ● ● ● ● ● ● ● ● ●

CONVERSATIONAL LATIN

All universities offer at least one course in a dead and COMPLETELY USELESS LANGUAGE. In Roman Studies 25: Conversational Latin, you will learn how to speak a dead and completely useless language.

You've just arrived in Rome and you're eager for a good time. First, you need wheels: QUANTUM EST PRAETIUM CARROS LOCANDAS? Now that you know how much a rented chariot will set you back you need more cash. UBI'S the word you need. UBI means where. UBI EST AMERICANUS EXPRESSUS? Great, you're mobile, and you're loaded with DISPUMPTI PERAGRANOREM—travelers checks! Wanna go shopping? Roma is the fashion capital of the empire so it's important to be well-dressed. QUANTUM EST PRAETIUM ILLA TOGA IN FENESTRA, or how much is that toga in the window? Take your new threads to the Forum Hotel and ask for a room with a view—CONTRA COLOSSEUM. Hungry? The TERBANA awaits. Thirsty? Just shout "VITUM SENATOR!" If you're traveling SOLUS, you must be getting lonely. Meeting people is a snap in Latin. Walk right up with a hearty "SALVE! QUOMODO VALLUS?" If the answer is "Fine. And you?" CARPE DIEM—seize the moment—and ask for a dance: "FISNE MECUM SALTARE." "NOLE ME IBI TANGERE" means "don't touch me there," but when they say enough talking—SATIS VERBORUM—and then "DOMUS MEA VEL DOMUS TUA"—my place or yours—you know you're going all the way, or "UMS QUEAT NAUSEUM". What a language! Now when you're back home you can say, "VENI, VIDI, VICI!" and mean it.

PHYSICS 183:

● ● ● ● ● ● ● ● ● ● ●

THE SPECIAL THEORY OF RELATIVITY

Physics is the study of ENERGY AND MATTER. In Physics 183, we will study the intellectually demanding Special Theory of Relativity. What makes it so special? Let's find out.

NEWTON was smart, but not that smart. It took EINSTEIN to straighten out space and time. Einstein may have failed long division, but how many people can say they figured out RELATIVITY? Einstein took LOREN's transformations and flipped the universe INSIDE OUT!

The important thing is C, see? C is another name for the SPEED OF LIGHT: 2.9979248 times 10^8 meters per second. That's fast, really fast! C is the same in all frames of reference for all observers. Wow, think about it! If a train is going ONE HUNDRED MILES PER HOUR and you run towards it at twenty miles an hour, you're not too bright, but you approach the train at around A HUNDRED AND TWENTY MILES AN HOUR, right? Now the engineer wonders who the idiot on the tracks is and turns on the headlights. The light's coming at you at C PLUS ONE HUNDRED AND TWENTY, right? Wrong! The light's still coming at you at plain old C, see? There's no absolute space or absolute time. TIME SLOWS DOWN AS YOU APPROACH THE SPEED OF LIGHT, see? T equals twice the square root of ET over 2 squared plus A squared all over C, see?

So a child on Earth ages faster than her ASTRONAUT mother traveling at near-C speeds, Mom comes home young, refreshed, little Betty looks like a prune. But relativity says that the faster you go, the MORE MASSIVE you become and the more you contract in length, so Mom's young, but she's short and fat, REAL FAT. And what is relevant about relativity? Plenty: it destroys your sense of space, trashes time, lambastes length, builds bombs, and makes the world a much more interesting place! Relatively speaking.

VISUAL ARTS 5:

● ● ● ● ● ● ● ● ● ● ● ●

FiLM
APPRECiATiON

Everybody knows how to watch a movie. In Visual Arts 5, we will learn how to APPRECiATE FiLM. **Lights please.**

Every film needs DIRECTION, and that's where the director comes in. A great director makes for a great film, like CITIZEN KANE, but let's look at one of my favorites, GODZILLA. Now that's directing. And what about editing? See if you can catch all 100 cuts used to kill Janet Leigh in PSYCHO. If HITCHCOCK used that many cuts, then editing must be important. And where would a film be without ACTORS? Nowhere, that's where. THE SEVENTH SEAL is a classic film with great acting, but let's take a look at ROCKY. Wow! What emotion! Put that together with good CINEMATOGRAPHY, which is just a fancy word for saying camera work, and you've got MOVIE MAGIC. Watch the silent classic THE GREAT TRAIN ROBBERY. Masterful. But wait—what about sound? Is sound important? You bet. How would you like to see THE WIZARD OF OZ without [cackle]? Or imagine the car chase in THE FRENCH CONNECTION without [crash]. Or what would TEXAS CHAINSAW MASSACRE be without [buzz]? Now that you know how to appreciate film, see if you can appreciate all the subtleties in one of my favorites, MONDO TOPLESS. Roll 'em. Now that's filmmaking at its best.

COMPARATIVE LITERATURE 15:

● ● ● ● ● ● ● ● ● ● ● ●

THEME AND STRUCTURE

Learning why one great book is just like every other great book is the key to understanding what great literature is all about. In Comparative Literature 15, we will compare all the great works of literature from the BIBLE to VALLEY OF THE DOLLS.

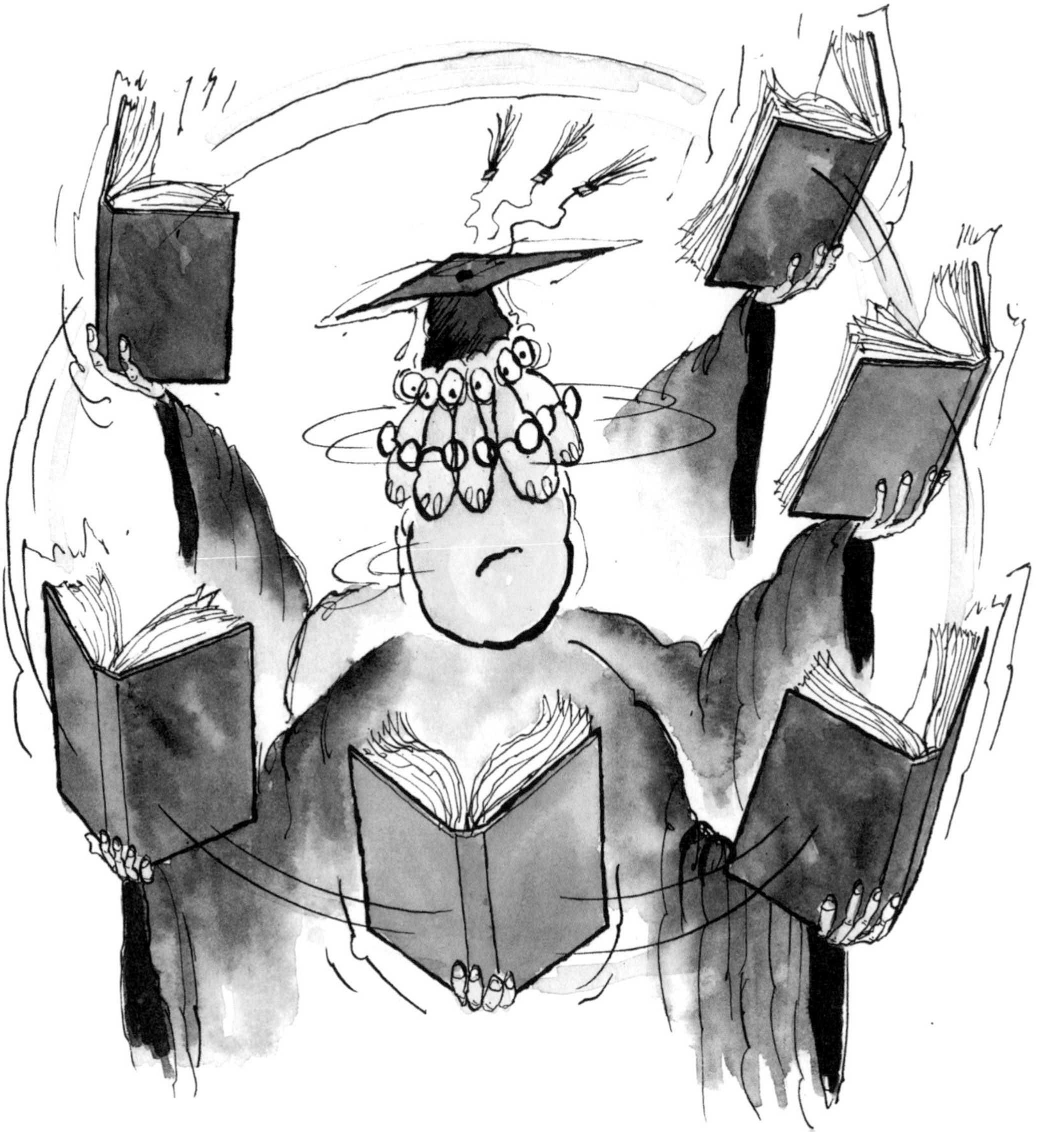

In the beginning, there was the Old Testament, which is just like the New Testament because they're both part of the Bible, which was written in verse just like THE ODYSSEY, which is exactly the same story as ULYSSES, which is long, real long just like GONE WITH THE WIND, which was later made into a really good movie just like ROMEO AND JULIET, which, even though it's a play, you can read just like a book just like NATIVE SON, which really is a book with lots of action just like THE ILLIAD, which also has lots of action just like TREASURE OF THE SIERRA MADRE, which has even more action, plus lots of horses, which were animals just like the animals in Orwell's ANIMAL FARM except they could talk just like those furry-footed hobbits in LORD OF THE RINGS, which sounds an awful lot like LORD OF THE FLIES in which my favorite character named Piggy reminds us again of Animal Farm, although Piggy dies, which is exactly what happens to most of the characters in CATCH 22, which is, after all, what you would expect from a war story like WAR AND PEACE, which for my money is exactly like MOBY DICK because they're both incredibly boring. That's what makes a great book great. Great like LADY CHATTERLEY'S LOVER, which is incredibly boring too, but at least it's got lots of sex, while DEATH IN VENICE has a little sex but lots of Italians like IACOCCA, and that one's pretty much the same as THE GREAT GATSBY because they're both about cars and money, which are things you can also find in DEATH OF A SALESMAN, which is actually a play just like HAMLET, which ends tragically just like A TALE OF TWO CITIES, which also ends in Europe just like MAGIC MOUNTAIN, which wasn't written in English just like Plato's THE REPUBLIC, which is an awful lot like VALLEY OF THE DOLLS because they're both great books.

ECONOMICS 2:

• • • • • • • • • • • •

THE MARKET SYSTEM

Did you ever wonder why Christmas cards go on sale the day after Christmas? SUPPLY AND DEMAND. This is Economics 2: The Market System.

So what is economics? Simple. Economics is the scientific inquiry and analysis of quantitative data pertaining to the allocation of SOCIETY'S CASH RESOURCES to produce and distribute the fruits of production as commodities for the consumption of individuals and groups that comprise a society, which means supply and demand. Take a look at BEETS. Say there's a big BUMPER CROP in beets. Everybody's got beets coming out their ears, and extra supply drives beets down to twenty-nine cents a pound. DEMAND GOES UP. So more people buy more beets, all things being equal or as we say in economics, SETORUS APPARABUS. But if BRUSSELS SPROUTS take a dive to nineteen cents a pound, people might opt for BRUSSELS OVER BEETS, and demand for beets bottoms out—unless beet and brussels buyers experience a per capita INCREASE IN INCOME. Then demand is up for both beets and brussels in this BOOM OR BUST BEET/BRUSSELS MARKET. But if the price of sour cream were to soar—and sour cream is a COMPLIMENTARY COMMODITY to the beet in the production of BORSCHT—then we'd see a shift in the beet demand curve to the left. Put that together with the high price elasticity of the demand for beets.

After all, do you really have to have a beet? Wouldn't a carrot or cuc do? And you'll have the beet lobby begging for beet subsidies. But then, out of nowhere, the Surgeon General announces, "BEETS CURE CANCER." A boom market develops in the beet market and when this dirty little vegetable goes through the roof at ten dollars a pound, you can bet everyone and their mother will be looking for a WINDFALL in beets. So where will beets be tomorrow? Beats me.

FOOTBALL:

● ● ● ● ● ● ● ● ● ● ●

THE GAME OF LIFE

"Got a minute?
Gonna win it!
Says who?
TMU! TMU!
That's who, that's who!
Gooooo team!"

At TMU we develop the BODY as well as the mind. And if college is anything, COLLEGE IS FOOTBALL. You have to think on your feet, play like a team player, and give it everything you've got.

Everyone, listen up. Football is a thinking man's game, so let's talk strategy. First things first. How do you tell friend from foe on the field? Look at the color of your shirt. Same color, same team. Different color, different team. OFFENSE, listen up. Say it's third and goal, ten seconds to go, and you smell a BLITZ. What do you do? SCREEN PASS to the sidelines to stop the clock, then the quarterbacks meet for six—no SPIKING. Now for the ritual BUTT SLAPPING and HELMET BASHING. Don't forget that extra point. DEFENSE, listen up. BIG GUYS line up in front, LITTLE GUYS in back, nobody moves. When the ball is snapped flat and those blockers SACK THE QB and strip out the ball and head for home, up goes another six points for good old TMU. Even if you get your BELL RUNG, keep the momentum going. Time is of the essence, so play like there's NO TOMORROW. Your SCHOLARSHIPS depend on it. What do you hear if you fumble out there? ["Booo!"] What do you want to hear? ["Yaaay!"] But the real music is the sound the NOSE GUARD makes when he hits the CENTER. Basic football. Physical football. It's a GAME OF INCHES, and we're out there for one reason and one reason only—to win! It's not a Sunday social. It's DOG EAT DOG, them or us. So when you're in the TRENCHES with 3000 pounds of defense making MINCEMEAT out of you, when they're shredding your blockers and intercepting your HAIL MARYS and sacking your boy in the snap, what are you gonna do? You're gonna get MEAN. You're gonna get TOUGH. You're gonna get PHYSICAL. You're gonna get out there and KILL!

COMMENCEMENT

As I take SEVERAL SECONDS to reflect, I can't help but think how quickly these ten minutes have passed. It seems like it was only but moments ago that I first welcomed you to TMU. As you go out into the world in pursuit of your careers—WHETHER IT BE IN FINANCE, NUCLEAR MEDICINE, PSYCHOANALYSIS, FAST FOOD, GENETIC RESEARCH, SANITATION, ENGINEERING, FOREIGN SERVICE, COMMUNICATIONS, EDUCATION, OR FOOTBALL—you will take with you the finest and most comprehensive education that one can possibly expect to receive in ten minutes. THE WORLD NEEDS YOU. Don't waste a second.